THROUGH WEATHERED TREES

Poetry by
DEAN S. HURLIMAN

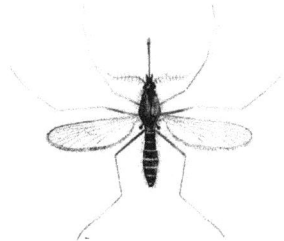

Zanzara Press

Zanzara Press
918 5TH ST
Ames, IA 50010
USA
zanzarapress.com
editor@zanzarapress.com

Zanzara Press

THROUGH WEATHERED TREES
2023 © Dean S. Hurliman

ISBN-13: 978-1-941892-62-6

Library of Congress Control Number: 2023935173

Book layout and design 2023 © by polytekton.com

This Book is dedicated to my son
John Alvin Hurliman, b. 1981

Of his many handicaps he's not aware:
blind, can't speak or walk
and yet he finds enjoyment here
and has no doubt that life is fair.
About him is an angel's glow;
and all he needs is love
and it will show.

Table of Contents

Power

Who has the most power upon this earth?
President? Tycoon?
or head of a church?
The despot in an evil regime?
Or one who runs the war machine?

It's none of these
but who has the means
to harness vocabulary,
turn men to machines.
If you can speak with a
lying vigor,
label "others" subhuman,
Untermensch, gook or nigger;
good people are led to abandon their neighbor.
And it's good people who
will pull the trigger.

Four Little Poems (all true)

Grant
General U. S. Grant
was a cultured man.
He liked good cigars
and he liked a good band.
"I know but two songs and that is sufficient.
"Yankee Doodle" is one.
The other one isn't".

Jim Thorpe (American Indian) 1912 Olympics, Stockholm
Jim Thorpe, "Bright Path", won the world class prize
dominating The Games to no one's surprise.
Despite all acclaim
he was unassuming.
Yet his name still has that golden ring.
When King Gustav of Sweden gave Jim great praise,
the shy reply was a terse "Thanks King".

Columbus Day Celebration
On Columbus Day 1992,
celebrating our culture
as a good citizen should
I gathered my collection of flint arrowheads
and solemnly placed them back in the woods.

Three Little Birds
Tres pájaros pequeños
esta en mi corazón,
pero no sé la razón,
cuando estoy trabajando
y cuando soñando.

My Dog Tad

I once had a dog
so trusting and grand
he would walk through a mesh fence
at my command.

*****

When Tad was a pup
we were at a ballpark.
I was throwing a ball in a
wide ranging arc.
One ball found its way
to the wrong side of the fence
but to Tad it made no difference.
In my command and judgment
he had confidence.
So lowering his head
tried to walk through the fence.

The Last Words of Copernicus

The last words of Copernicus
just before he died:
"I stand by all my theories
(Oh the trouble truth can cause)
Yet it's painful to bear witness
When two spheres collide.'

'The sun is at the center
the planets are in tow.
Equants and epicycles
are misguided astral show.
Perception mirrors reality
but does not make it so.

'Science stands all by itself
without the help of God.
As a true believer in the Church,
I pray Rome will not fade:
glowing bright
as the moon in perigee
or Mars in retrograde."

Iowa

These fields of soybeans, proud and grand,
fields of corn, neatly planned, now grow
on what was prairie land.

The bygone eden of the big bluestem
sways to a tall grass requiem
for a catalog of midwest flowers.

Gone like sudden summer showers;
a heritage of species shorn
some with us still, some lost, unknown.

Iowa's soil - rich and dark
was once an open rangeland park.
In time such diversity,
was victim of its own fertility,
a classic prairie treasury
turned modern trilogy:
beans, corn, humanity.

Giving

The hungry dog you just fed
the child you just held,
they don't give a damn
of vain glory in your head.

Heaven takes care of its cares
God's grace will open doors
for those who share but little
or those who man the oars.
It's here on earth
that good works count.
It's here we keep a score.

A widow's mite is fine in heaven
but not so here on earth.
Great accolades and rightly so
To those who fill the purse.

The motive of your charity
might be publicity driven;
don't disregard your vanity.
Accept the flattery.
Be useful to humanity.
No praise for what you have.
Praise for what you've given.

The Bridge

There is a bridge no longer used,
it's underwater now.
Before there were First Nations
First Peoples wandered there
and challenged a new continent with
flint tipped wooden spears.

How quaint and innocent the tools,
in some collectors hand
and yet they were essential
to those small restless bands.
The first to use an implement
to work their will
on New World land.

First Peoples
did not scar the land
they lacked the wherewithal.
In decades what they built
would melt into the soil
scarce noticed if at all.
Their great achievement:
use the land -
but make your impact
slight and small.

Whiteness

Consider white things
God has made:
a summer cloud, a bank of snow,
a pigeon's wing.

Not pure, not perfect pure.
Marred by shadow, stain or lines of age
as white pine are.

Perhaps the world demands
a perfect tablecloth of tatted lace.
It's Devil's work expecting purity
from someone's face.

Purity is something
God seldom did bestow.
So much for white as perfect,
not much has been created so.

Cattle and Men

When understanding cattle and men
here's the key:
We see the blank eyes empty and dumb;
the self contented
chewing their cud.
Not bred for wisdom-
but neither are we.

Late August

Late August now,
all color abloom,
a wildness of flowers
reminiscent of June,
with excited cicadas
loud and ceaseless at noon.

We are wrapped in discomfort,
like a monarch's cocoon,
in an open air sweatlodge
of percussion and heat.
A droning duet
that fills up a room
in my heart with the gloom
of unease and regret;
of vague tasks left undone
and life passing too soon.

But the wind has not
changed yet,
not a hint in its tune,
of dread winter coming
with its cold arctic moon.

Revel then in each warm day
and those left to come.
Sing with the cicadas,
feel the beat of their drum.
And All.
All around you.
Emerging as One.

The Wood

I sat a while in a quiet wood
and blended in as
best I could;
and fancied here would
be all ease
to be a part of
such as these.

However, in this
simple glade
there came unease,
a troubling sense.
Mankind's not made
for innocence.
We yearn to fit
yet remain,
aloof observers
in the shade.

Favored Ancients

Those favored ancient peoples
who lived among the gods;
how must a wonder filled their lives
to wander where the sacred trod.

Faded away are ancients now,
but not the art they drew;
rock wall gods remain on earth,
(lion, bear and kangaroo).

What irony this modern age
at odds
with sacred worth.
Its mission now:
preserve the gods,
alive and with us,
still on earth.

Mercy

In doling out perfection
God was circumspect:
the young, the handicapped,
all mentally beleaguered souls who
never win.
The rest of us were made to sin
it's what we do.
And yet.
This one allowance:
repent and by some miracle of grace
be heaven sent.

You unrepentant with a list of small delinquencies
God will shrug his shoulders,
(I suspect)
curse beneath his breath,
and also let you in.

Rookie Baseball

Squint rookie.
Look into the sun;
with unbelieving eyes
at lightning fastballs
swift as bullets from a gun.

Glide rookie.
Snag the long hit ball;
pirouette across the grassy stage as if
in some grand music hall.

Sprint rookie.
Bound like the tireless deer
whose well worn game path leads
to home
where rivals afield await you there.

Play rookie.
Cavort as if forever young;
error free with ease and victory
over all opponents,
every one.

Run rookie.
Be never tamed;
a carefree, shoeless
summer child
in a schoolyard pick-up game.

The Heath Hen's Tale

Becca Dustman (hired girl)
"Well I must say they're underfoot
as common anywhere
as fleas upon a feather bed.
I do declare.
Served a bird six days a week!
I've had enough of them to eat.
I'm pleased when Friday rolls around
and cook can serve no meat."

Most Reverend Portman (self-titled pastor)
"Praise and blessings upon you brethren as says The Sacred Book!
God doth provide abundance everywhere you look! I must confess there seems a bird
in every nook! Best served with wine or beer! The birds are done and ready so
says the cook! Your treat! Get out your pocketbook! Just look! In Chapter One as
says The Sacred Book, "Mankind shall rule the earth and do just as he please!"
What a blessing- pleasing God by eating such as these!"

Mr. Dollard (business man)
"To buy and sell, that is my trade.
When things get scarce I'll raise the price.
If hens should disappear I won't think twice.
There's plenty a songbird will suffice.
Or a deal in Golden Eagles would be nice."

Ben Mather (scientist)
"There's really nothing to be done.
Nature has its way,
and we must stand aside
and let her have her say.
Excuse me, I must grab my gun.
I'm off pursuing specimens;
collecting disappearing birds
for the new Smithsonian."

Dreams

Of all dreams I've ever had
the finest ones are these.

In the backyard of my childhood
gazing up through weathered trees,
high in a sky of fierce deep blue,
so high the eye can scarcely see,
are scores of birds
in flocks or solitary.
Hawks, snow geese and sandhill cranes
some known and others without names.
Their easy glide and mid- air pause
are done with such an ease;
there is no search for primal cause.
They exist only To Be.
I stand transfixed in ecstasy
of the world beyond the trees
and the freedom that surrounds me;
in the quiet of a humdrum life
shackled to the ground.

Buffalo Bill

The last of the buffalo Bill Cody killed
confirmed his status as a railroad shill.
The mayhem he caused is with us still;
but it's widely believed he was doing God's will.

When Custer last heard "Garryowen",
the tune marked the end of the military showman.
He knew heaven awaited, he'd not be forgot
for all the infidels he had shot.

Slavery, a scourge of the "civilized west"
is with us still; not yet put to rest.
We should mimic the slave owner and do our best
to uphold our convictions
with fanatical zest.

*****

For evil how wonderfully carefree an age.
from extinction to genocide,
still honored,
the graves
of the wicked ones
thought pure and brave.
No moral compunction, no prayers of outrage,
bad religion, bad action,
share the same page.

To A Dying Elephant

A soothing sonata
once was played,
as a kind farewell
to an old elephant
who shuffled in silence
then raised his trunk;
perhaps as a signal he forgave
those who
chained him
for circus parades.

I'm awed by the graciousness
the great beast displayed
before lumbering off to his
potter's field grave.

****

How true to form the most vicious on earth
keep the kind and the gentle
in chains
for their mirth.

Wisdom

Wisdom is ours when we understand
how quickly possessions fall from our hands;
we question their worth, the fuss and the bother.
At the end of the day all we have is each other.

Rain

You walk outside and it sure smells like rain;
the wind and the Spring leaves wrestle again
while the dogs from the countryside tumble around.
Blue jays are calling
and in the background
a woodpecker drills with its distinctive sound.
The squirrels are displeased
and happily so.
The air's damp and warm and you hear mushrooms grow.
It's a snapshot of Nature,
a world all aglow.

But here's a sad secret
you regretfully know:
despite all around being family and kin
you remain on the outside.
You'll never fit in.

Dog Dreams

It seems my dog
has pleasant dreams,
the muffled bark,
the twitching feet.
He pursues a life of joy
even in his sleep.

There's a message here
for all to hear,
though it helps to understand
Dogspeak.

Be relentless in
pursuing joy,
even in your sleep.

October

There is something afoot in October
a mystery occurring each fall.
We are left behind to fend as we may
to watch and wonder at it all.

It's a migration of life
that clears the skies
of much we esteem,
much that we prize.

The morning song,
the midnight call
gone 'til
Spring's awakening comes along.

We'll never get enough of fall,
because we love yet understand
but little of it all.

Scotland County Coon Hunters Assn.

Rutledge, Missouri 1977

Hoodoos appear in their
dog dreams tonight.
You can hear the hounds baying
with wild delight;
the woods filled with music
thrilling to hear.
Each dog's in a world forever vexed;
if no track is struck
"Hie on!" to the next.
Old men with their small talk are gathering here,
jack knives in their pockets
their hand on a beer;
leather lined faces ogre like in the glare
from an oak, hickory campfire,
aflame with the flares
of a sweet smoky odor which hangs in the air.
Others step to the woods and soon disappear
pints of clear moonshine awaiting them there.
They speak of their hounds
with a softness you feel.
Approach them with reverence; all gathered here
at first glance they may appear simple, sincere.
But do not underestimate them or their peers

.

A full moon is rising, dogs track where they're led
by a canine enigma loose in their heads.
Out there is a mystery
one cannot perceive;
yet baying hounds sense it with animal ease.
Oh, friend, we are that baying hound
guided by a breeze.
A mad howl through the dark unknown;
at the close of the hunt we'll ache to the bone.
A vague end ahead of us, never in sight,
while the Old Man of the Shadows
follows our flight .

Snow Storms

I've quite a liking for a storm
with large flakes
of snow
that blows hard
but does not accumulate;
that leaves no towering drifts
when weather breaks.

So many times I'm left to speculate
on some worrying,
fretful incident,
that seemingly besets me so,
but ends
a trivial event,
like storms with large flaked snow.

Heat Lightning

As children abed
on the old sleeping porch,
it was thrilling to see as darkness
approached
thunderheads massing
down south
downriver
with each passing moment
the anvil got bigger;
'till at last clouds were lit
again and again
by a silent light flashing
that came from within.
"Heat Lightning" we'd whisper
and know we were right,
so safe in that wisdom,
snuggle deep in our covers
and sleep for the night.

Mars Landing

When mankind finally lands on Mars
handing Peace Medals
to the high and low,
I hope the Martians understand
the meaning of the gift bestowed.
"This is ours.
We own it now.
You'll have to go."

Earth's Downfall

What if mankind got it wrong from the start?
By what dark art or lack of sense
were we brought to this precipice?

When old King Lear decided to retire
and split the kingdom among his daughters,
he'd no idea what would happen hence.
So too mankind must deal
with unintended consequence.
How can ideas with beginnings so small
in the end be the cause of the earth's downfall?

Genesis bestows a theological prop
to the "image of God"
to stay on top.
How convenient is this holy writ.
Our share of the loaf is..... all of it.
Capitalism has a grip of gold
wealths' acquisition is admired, adored.
The ledger always off a bit;
from the earth, take a little
more of it.
Lastly, and causing the most distress,
(in doubt of all things but itself).
Science.

New king of kings and lord of lords
by its own fiat the final word.
But the science project has run amok;
natural disasters wherever you look.
Morality set us on this course.
Can amorality save us from ourselves?
"I looked, and behold a pale horse."

As for science, our savior,
let me be Frank,
"Don't expect Jesse James
to bring gold to a bank".

The Natural World

There's a barrier of fate
that keeps we humans separate
from the natural world around us
we long to integrate.

We try but it is evident
these worlds are incompatible.
Every time the landscape's changed
the world becomes unstable.

Surely, God or evolution
has done us some great wrong;
We've slipped the trace of understanding
Nature's joyous All Day song.

Whirlwinds

Those wandering little whirlwinds?
Once Zephyrus paused to let me in.
An aerial cotillion in a field of corn
remnants of harvest whirling around.
The west wind took my spirit
airborne
free, ether-light
from the tight gripping ground.
Aloft in a tower
of nothing but air;
nothing but freedom
holding me there.

*****

Now and then free your spirit
from the here and the now.
Make it your aim
to play with the gods.
Invite yourself into their games.
Flirt with a goddess,
let her know you by name.
Fill your dance card with improv
avoid gravity;
soon enough it will hold us
for eternity.

The Leaf

I'd like to see a worn out leaf
still clinging to its place
upon a twig;
then wait for wind
and seeing its release
race
and try to catch it
before it hits the ground.
To praise it not for color
but because it should be known
that service to the earth
has a beauty all its own.

Johnny Platt

A small old man in baggy pants
who pushed a squeaky two wheel cart
down hollyhock lined alleys
rummaging for metal scraps.

Or perhaps a ripe tomato
growing through the fence.
The neighborhood was easy
with great abundance.

He did not comprehend
the war was won;
the need for saving every scrap was done.
But scavenging was something he could do.
The little money earned
would help his aged mother
see him through.

His appearance was a treasure trove
of maladies as from the Book of Job:
eyes were crossed, voice a rasp,
shaking hands,
a motley colored skin like Joseph's robe.
One long, and short sleeve shirt
and winter coat were all he seemed to own.

Yearly he'd show on the very date,
when Alice turned six or seven or eight,
to hang about the garden gate
where Mom would bring him on a plate
a glass of milk and birthday cake.
And all of us would celebrate.

When I think back on my childhood's glow
it's folks like Johnny
that made it so.

The Storm

Far off to the west
a boom and a crash.
Storm clouds are massing.
Happening fast.
Wind's picked up.
Sky's turning green.
The county's a battleground;
clouds burst
on the scene.
It's war in the sky
of two atmospheres.
A great cosmic joust:
cold air from the north meets warm air from the south.
The fields and the gardens
are dry as a bone;
the rains are welcome,
and can't come too soon.
The duel in the heavens
will give rise to new birth.
It's a clash of the Titans
that benefits earth.

Blackberry Pie

There's a wooded glen
just over the road,
by Aunt Clara's farm
where in hottest July
blackberries grow bold,
laughing and preening
among their thorns,
waiting for picking
in the dew humid morn.

Here Mildred and Eunice
spent many a damp hour,
dressed in straw hats and ragged attire
enduring those thorns
or a brief morning shower,
gathering a harvest
to glorify
later that evening when chores were laid by
the essence of summer;
homemade blackberry pie.

Handicapped

All suffering handicapped
and others such as these,
all those in constant darkness and those under siege,
all abused ones, those living with strife,
those labeled unwanted
with no birthing date
gone with the blessing of the state.
All persons unlike we
who ease through life
self satisfied,
seemingly of higher grade.
Here's news.
In value none was ever made
unequal, undeserving.
Everyone's a masterpiece.
So surely it must please the Lord
to grant indulgence on
release.

Furthermore, the heaven that awaits them
must be so rich in joy and mirth
to compensate for all they missed on earth.
It is with hope they find it so and we've not been misled.
I pray that God is just as kind
as all the Gospels said.

Rides-Away-Twinkling

There's a tall grass meadow
close by our woods.
One day on a hike I stopped and I stood
listening to sounds in the neighborhood.
Far off from nowhere
came the jingling of bells;
it was Rides-Away-Twinkling
from a child's dell.
Both long time forgotten
yet remembered well.

A young Indian girl
on a large Appaloosa
with star shiny bells
all round her neck.
Her leggings aglitter
with trade beads
bedecked; she turned
in the saddle and her shy smile asked,
if we'd ride together
as we'd done in the past.
(What confidence the young girl had
to ride the prairies far from home
and call the endless horizon her own!)

My answer a sad one,
a lost, older look.
Alone she rode back,
as she'd done in my youth,
to the tattered and torn of
a childhood book.

My Father

My father had two life long dreams
and both were unfulfilled.

He yearned to farm
a fallow field,
so yearly leased an acreage
sufficient for our pantry
and the neighborhood.

Yet, he often stood
at furrows end
and dreamed of might have beens.
But trading dreams for children
he could not take a chance,
on the vagaries of farm finance and so remained
an antiwar machinist
at the Iowa Ordnance Plant.

I heard an earnest prayer one night
"Let me be born again".
But he was born a Lutheran.
Surely he'd be ushered in
to the Kingdom and be washed of sin?

Verily, verily it's a two way street
for religion to make life good:
it must not make demands
which cannot be understood.

Mother's Daydream

My mother had a railroad pass,
back in the Age of Steam
Her father worked on the CB&Q;
she used it quite extensively
to fulfill her yearning teenage dreams
of freedom,
on a trip to Denver
in 1923;
or Uncle Cooksey's dirt poor farm
in now lost Dean and Sedan Bottoms
in hardscrabble Appanoose County.

No wonder in those later years
I'd find her on the porch,
worn out pulling weeds in the garden patch,
an apron full of beans to snap,
with eyes closed, swinging gently,
humming a well known gospel verse,
daydreaming of a railroad coach
on the Front Range of the Rockies,
traveling unchaperoned,
alone and free.
All by herself.

The Flood of Alexandria, Missouri, 1993

There's a pall of smoke o'er the river's floodplain
where the Mississippi has lived up to its name
to top the doorways and window panes
of Alexandria now set aflame
to clear the rubble of the river's campaign.
The scene looks Medieval with fires and stench.
Both stalwart and stunned now gather 'round trenches
where sodden lumber from churches and dwellings
burns into the night
steaming and hissing
with tall tales of escape
as common as
flooding.

The drama's man made with shovels and dredges
when levees narrow river edges
forcing a natural water rise
to breach a levee without compromise.
We've yet to learn this easy lesson;
the wider the floodplain,
the greater the blessing.

www.ingramcontent.com/pod-product-compliance
Lightning Source LLC
Chambersburg PA
CBHW080020280326
41934CB00015B/3419